Roemarie Lang

This second book in the MASTER COMPREHENSION series teaches chil... variety of essential comprehension skills that help them underst... t they have read. The book's short, simple paragraphs about ga... s of interest to younger children will capture their interest and h... The 8 skills covered in the paragraphs and short stories are liste...

Table of Contents

continued next page

Table of Contents (continued)

Skills Glossary

Classifying. Putting things that are alike into categories.

Comprehension. Understanding what is read.

Following Directions. Doing what the directions say to do.

Inference. Using logic to figure out what is unspoken but evident.

Main Idea. Finding the most important points.

Predicting Outcome. Telling what is likely to happen based on available facts.

Same/Different. Being able to tell how things are the same and different.

Sequencing. Putting things in order.

Name: _____

Cats Like Milk

Directions: Read about what cats like. Then predict what they will do.

Cats like milk. Do you? Set out a pan of juice. Set out a pan of milk.

1. What will a cat do?

_____

_____

2. Why?

_____

_____

3. Color the cat's dish.

Playful Cats

Directions: Read about cats.
Then follow the instructions.

Cats make good pets.
They like to play.
They like to jump.
They like to run. Do you?

1. Cats make good   pets.

                 friends.

2. Name 3 things cats like to do:

1) _____

2) _____

3) _____

3. Think of a name for a cat. Write it on the cat's tag.

4

Name: _____

A Game For Cats

Directions: Read about what cats like. Then follow the instructions.

Cats like to play with paper bags. Pull a paper bag open. Take everything out. Now lay it on its side.

1. Put the pictures in 1, 2, 3 order.

2. In 4, draw what you think the cat will do.

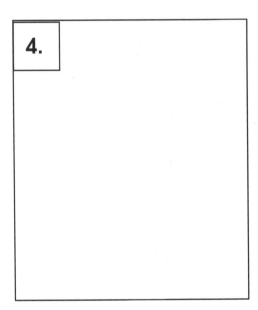

4.

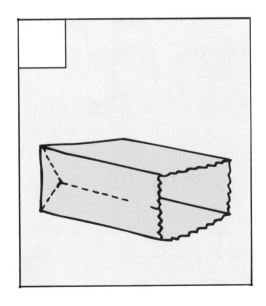

Name: _____

Pretty Parrots

Directions: Read about parrots. Then follow the instructions.

Big parrots are pretty. Their feet each have four toes. Two toes are in front. Two toes are in back. Parrots use their feet to climb. They use them to hold food.

1. A parrot's foot has   4 toes.

                             2 toes.

2. Name 2 things a parrot does with his feet.

1) _____   2) _____

3. Color the parrot.

Name: _____

Parrot Art

Directions: Draw the parts that are missing on each parrot.

1. Draw the parrot's EYE.   2. Draw the parrot's TAIL.

3. Draw the parrot's BEAK.   4. Draw the parrot's WINGS.

Name: _____

Dirty Dogs

Directions: Read about dogs. Then follow the instructions.

Like people, dogs get dirty. Some dogs get a bath once a month. Baby soap is a good soap for cleaning dogs. Fill a tub with warm water. Get someone to hold the dog still in the tub. Then wash the dog fast.

1. How often do some dogs get a bath?

_____

_____

_____

2. What is a good soap to use on dogs?

_____

_____

_____

3. Do you think most dogs like to take baths?

_____

_____

_____

Dog-gone!

Directions: Read the story. Then follow the instructions.

Ben and Ann were washing Spot. His fur was wet. Their hands were wet. Spot did NOT like to be wet. Ben dropped the soap. Ann picked it up and let go of Spot. Uh-oh!

1. Tell what happened next.

_____

_____

_____

_____

_____

2. Draw what happened next.

Name: _____

Review

Directions: Read about how to move the goldfish. Then follow the instructions.

Here is how to move a goldfish into a new bowl:

1. Fill the new bowl with fresh water.
2. Put the net under the fish and lift it from the old bowl.
3. Turn the net upside down. Close your hand over the net so the fish can't jump out.
4. Turn the net upside down over the fresh bowl of water. Let the fish drop in.

1. Number the pictures in 1, 2, 3, 4 order.

2. In your own words, tell someone how to move a goldfish into a new bowl.

_____

_____

_____

_____

_____

_____

3. Predict what could happen if you DID NOT close your hand over the net in step 3.

_____

_____

_____

Name: _____

Find The Puppets

Directions: Read about puppets. Then follow the instructions.

There are many kinds of puppets. Some puppets fit on your hand. Some puppets fit on your fingers. Some puppets are moved by strings.

Find and color the 3 puppets on this page. What kind of puppets did you find?

1. _____ 2. _____ 3. _____

Name: _____

Paper Sack Puppets

Directions: Read about paper sack puppets. Then follow the instructions.

It is easy to make a hand puppet. You need a small sack. You need colored paper. You need glue. You need scissors. Are you ready?

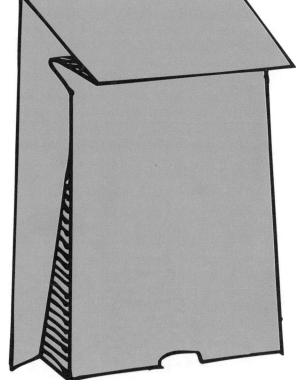

1. The main idea is:

   You need scissors.

   Making a hand puppet is easy.

2. What 4 things do you need to make a paper sack puppet?

   1) _____ 2) _____

   3) _____ 4) _____

3. Draw a face on the paper sack puppet.

Name: _____

Make A Paper Sack Puppet

Directions: Read how to make a paper sack puppet. Then follow the instructions.

 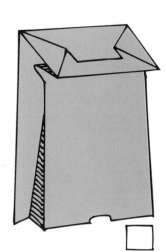

Find a small sack that fits your hand. Make a face where the sack folds. Cut out teeth from colored paper. Glue them on the sack. Cut out ears. Cut out a nose. Cut out a mouth. Glue them all on.

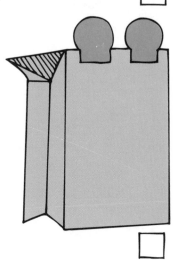 

1. What will you cut out first? _____

_____

2. What will you cut out last? _____

_____

3. Number the steps in 1, 2, 3, 4 order.

New Cards From Old

Directions: Read about making cards. Then answer the questions.

Did you ever get a card? Do you still have it? You can use it to make a new card. Then you can give the new card away.

1. What can you use to make a new card?

_____

_____

2. What can you do with the new card?

_____

_____

3. Who can you give a card to?

_____

_____

_____

Name: _____

Making A Card

Directions: Read about how to make a card. Then follow the instructions.

You will need scissors and glue. Find some colored paper. First, look at all your old cards. Then, cut out what you like. Now, fold the colored paper in half. Glue onto the front what you have cut out. Write your name inside.

Tell in order the steps for making a card.

1. Look at all your old cards.

_____

2. _____

_____

_____

3. _____

_____

_____

4. _____

_____

5. Write your name inside.

Draw a picture of a new card you could make.

Name: _____

Types Of Tops

Directions: Read about tops. Then answer the questions.

Tops come in all sizes. Some tops are made of wood. Some tops are made of tin. All tops do the same thing. They spin! Do you have a top?

1. The main idea is:

   There are many kinds of tops.

   Some tops are made of wood.

2. What are some tops made of?

   _____

   _____

   _____

   _____

3. What do all tops do?

   _____

   _____

Name: _____

Inference: Tops

Directions: Read about the girl's top. Then follow the instructions.

A girl gets a new top. She wants it put up where it is safe. She asks her dad to put it up high. Where can her dad put it?

1. Tell where the girl's dad can put the top.

_____

_____

_____

2. Draw a place the girl's dad can put the top.

Review

Directions: Read about making clay. Then follow the instructions.

It is fun to work with clay. Here is what you need to make it:

1 cup salt   2 cups flour   3/4 cup water

Mix the salt and flour. Then add the water.
Do NOT eat the clay. It tastes bad.
Use your hands to mix and mix.
Now roll it out. What can you make?

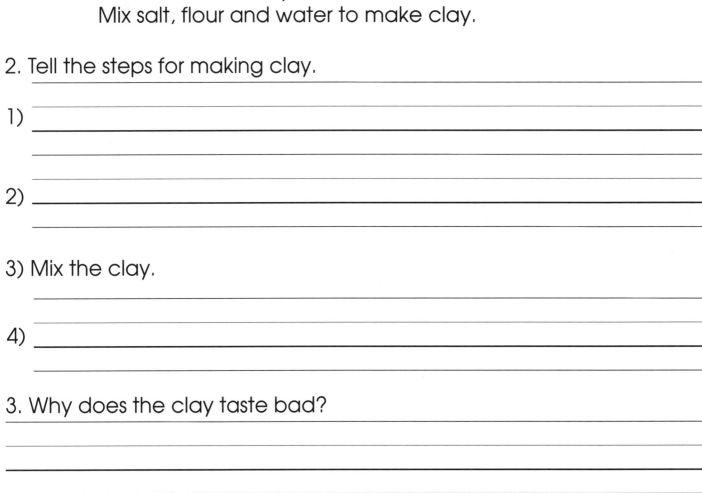

1. The main idea is:

      Do not eat this clay.

      Mix salt, flour and water to make clay.

2. Tell the steps for making clay.

1) _____

_____

_____

2) _____

_____

3) Mix the clay.

_____

4) _____

_____

3. Why does the clay taste bad?

_____

_____

_____

Name: _____

Using Tools

Directions: Read about art tools. Then color only the art tools.

You need tools for art. To cut, you need scissors. To draw, you need a pencil. To color, you need a crayon. To paint, you need a brush.

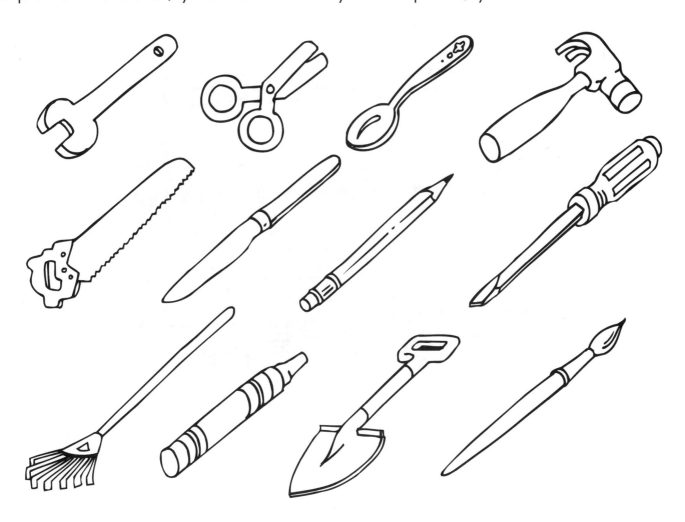

1. Tell what tools are needed to:

draw
_____
_____
_____

color
_____
_____
_____

cut
_____
_____
_____

Name: _____

About Ant Farms

Directions: Read about ant farms. Then answer the questions.

Ant farms are sold at toy stores and pet stores. Ant farms come in a flat frame. The frame has glass on each side. Inside the glass is sand. The ants live in the sand.

1. Where are ant farms sold?

_____   _____

_____   _____

_____   _____

_____   _____

2. The ants live in

             glass.   sand.

3. The ant farm frame is

             flat.   round.

Name: _____

Down On The Ant Farm

Directions: Read about ants. Then follow the instructions.

Ants are busy on the farm. They dig in the sand. They make roads in the sand. They look for food in the sand. When an ant dies, other ants bury it.

1. Where do you think ants are buried?

_____

_____

_____

2. Is it fair to say ants are lazy?

_____

_____

_____

3. Write a word that tells about ants. _____

_____

_____

_____

Name: _____

Just Junk?

Directions: Read about junk. Then follow the instructions.

Do you save old crayons? Do you save old buttons or cards? Some kids call these things junk. They throw them out. Some kids save these things. They put them in a box. What do you do?

The main idea is:

Everyone has junk.

People have different
ideas about what junk is.

1. Name 2 kinds of "junk."

1) _____

_____

2) _____

_____

2. What are 2 things to do with junk?

1) _____

_____

2) _____

_____

Name: _____

Color The Junk

Directions: Color the buttons red. Color the jacks silver. Color the crayon green. Draw and color some of your "junk."

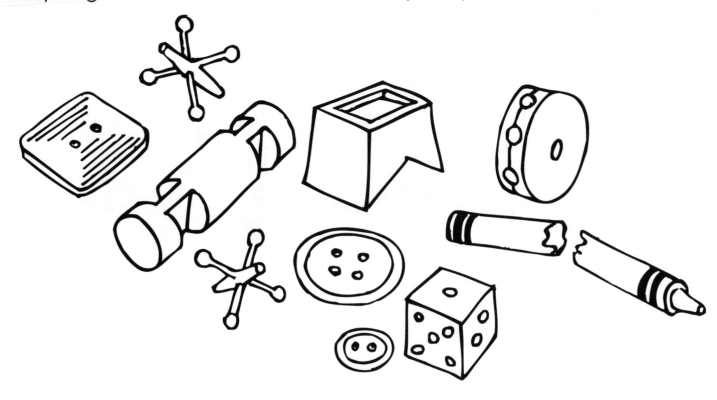

Draw your
junk here ⇨

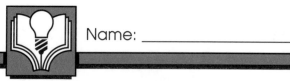

Name: _____

Playing Store

Directions: Read about playing store. Then follow the directions.

Some kids like to play store. They use boxes and cans. They line them up. Then they put them in bags.

1. The main idea is:

   Kids use boxes, cans and bags to play store.

   You need bags to play store.

2. Who likes to play store?

   All kids

   Some kids

3. Do you like to play store?

_____

_____

_____

Name: _____

Packing Bags

Directions: Read about putting things in bags. Then number in 1-2-3-4 order the way to do it.

Cans are heavy. Put them in first. Then put in boxes. Now put in the apple. Put the bread in last.

Name: _____

Review

Directions: Read the story. Then answer the questions.

Ann has many books. Some of Ann's books are about dogs. Some are about games. Some are about plants. Ann wants a pet. She reads about it in one of her books.

1. The main idea is:

    Ann learns things from books.

    Ann likes games.

2. Would you classify Ann as:

    A person who likes to read.

    A person who does not like to read.

3. What kind of pet does Ann want?

_____

_____

_____

4. Give directions on one way to learn about pets.

_____

_____

_____

Name: _____

Do You Like Jokes?

Directions: Read about jokes. Then follow the instructions.

Most kids like jokes. Some jokes are long. Some jokes are short. Good jokes are funny. Do you know a funny joke?

1. The main idea is:

    There are many kinds of jokes.

    Some jokes are short.

2. What did the rug say to the floor?

    _____

    _____

    _____

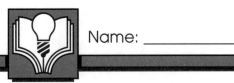

Name: _____

Letter Jokes

Directions: Draw the answers to the jokes.
Tell a joke you know.

Here are some jokes about letters.
What letter is part of the face? I (eye).
What letter can buzz? B (bee).

Did you hear the one about the buzzing letter?

1. Draw the answer to the letter I joke.

2. Draw the answer to the letter B joke.

3. Tell a joke you know.

_____

_____

_____

_____

_____

Name: _____

Color And Number Jokes

Directions: Read about jokes. Then answer the questions.

Here are more jokes! Do you know what color is loud? Do you know what number is not hungry?

1. The color that is loud is   PURple.   YELLow.

2. The number that is not hungry is   8.   2.

3. Here is one more joke. What color do you say when you are done with a book.

_____

"I have _____ it all."

A Winter Story

Directions: Read the story. Then answer the questions.

It is cold in winter. Snow falls. Water freezes. Most kids like to play outdoors. Some kids make a snowman. Some kids skate. What do you do in winter?

1. The main idea is:

   Snow falls in winter.

   In winter, there are many things to do outside.

2. Tell 2 things about winter weather.

   _____

   1) _____

   _____

   2) _____

   _____

3. Tell what you like to do in winter.

   _____

   _____

   _____

Making A Snowman

Directions: Read the story. Then follow the instructions.

It is fun to make a snowman. First, find things for the snowman's eyes and nose. Dress warmly. Then go outdoors. Roll a big snowball. Then roll another to put on top of it. Now roll a small snowball for the head. Put on the snowman's face.

1. Name 2 things to do before going outdoors.

1) _____

_____

2) _____

_____

2. Number the steps in the right order.

A Rainy Day

Directions: Read the story. Circle the things Lee needs to stay dry.

It is raining. Lee wants to play outdoors. What should he wear to stay dry? What should he carry to stay dry?

Name: _____

Following Directions: Baking A Cake

Directions: Read the story. Then give directions on how to bake a cake.

Ann, Lee and Dad will bake a cake. Dad turns on the oven. Ann opens the cake mix. Lee adds the eggs. Dad pours in the water. Ann stirs it. Lee pours the batter into a cake pan. Dad puts it in the oven.

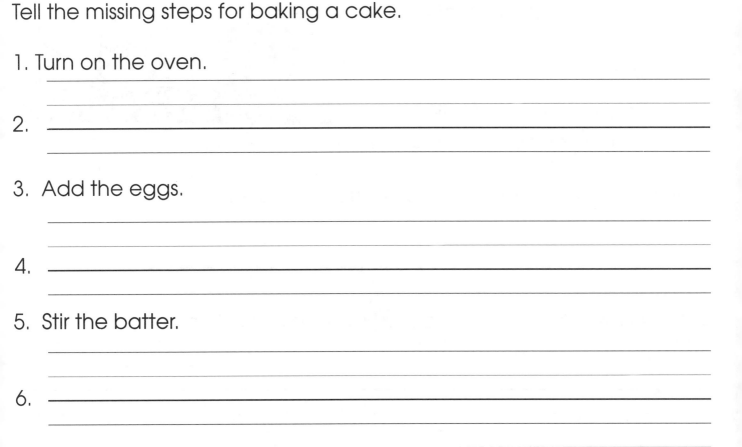

Tell the missing steps for baking a cake.

1. Turn on the oven.

2. _____

3. Add the eggs.

4. _____

5. Stir the batter.

6. _____

7. _____

Name: _____

Review

Directions: Read the story. Then follow the instructions.

The cake is done. It is taken from the oven. Ann and Lee want to frost it. "I want to use this white frosting," says Ann. "I want to use my red frosting," says Lee. "We will use both your ideas," says Dad. "We will have pink frosting."

1. The main idea is:

   The cake will have red frosting.

   Pink frosting is made of red and white.

2. The cake will be frosted

   after it is taken from the oven.

   before it is taken from the oven.

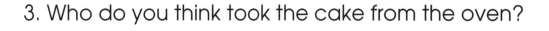

3. Who do you think took the cake from the oven?

   _____

   _____

   _____

4. Give directions on how Dad will make pink frosting.

   _____

   _____

   _____

5. Cakes are classified as:

   Sweets

   Fruits

Bluebirds And Parrots

Directions: Read about parrots and bluebirds. Tell how they are the same and different.

Bluebirds and parrots are both birds. Bluebirds and parrots can fly. They both have beaks. Parrots can live inside a cage. Bluebirds must live outdoors.

1. Tell 2 ways bluebirds and parrots are the same.

_____

1) _____

_____

2) _____

_____

2. Tell one way these birds are different.

Bluebirds must live _____

_____

_____

Parrots can live _____

_____

_____

Name: _____

Tigers

Directions: Read the story. Follow the instructions.

Tigers grow to be big! Some grow to be 10 feet long. Baby tigers are called cubs. They are small.

1. The main idea is:

    All tigers are big.

    Grownup tigers are big. Baby tigers are small.

2. What is a baby tiger called?

_____

_____

_____

_____

3. Color the tiger.

Name: _____

Cats And Tigers

Directions: Read about cats and tigers. Tell how they are the same and different.

Tigers are a kind of cat. Pet cats and tigers both have fur. Pet cats are small and tame. Tigers are large and wild.

1. Tell 1 way pet cats and tigers are the same.

_____

_____

_____

2. Tell 2 ways they are different:

Pet cats are small. Tigers are _____ .

_____

_____

Tigers are wild. Pet cats are _____ .

_____

37

Fish

Directions: Read about fish. Then follow the instructions.

Some fish live in warm water. Some live in cold water. Some fish live in lakes. Some fish live in oceans. There are 20,000 kinds of fish!

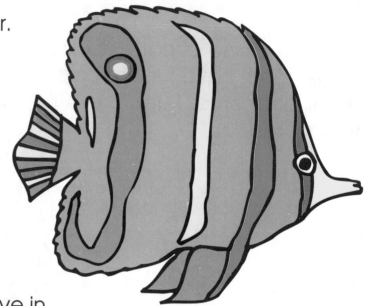

1. Name 2 types of water fish live in.

1) _____

2) _____

2. Name another place all fish live.

Some fish live in lakes and some live in _____ .

3. There are _____ kinds of fish.

Name: _____

Fish Come In Many Colors

Directions: Read about the color of fish. Then tell the colors and color the fish.

All fish live in water. Fish that live at the top are blue, green or black. Fish that live down deep are silver or red. The colors make it hard to see the fish.

1. Name 3 colors for fish at the top.

_____   _____   _____

_____   _____   _____

_____   _____   _____

2. Name 2 colors for fish that live down deep.

_____   _____

_____   _____

_____   _____

3. Color the top fish and the bottom fish the right colors.

Just Ducky

Directions: Read about ducks. Then answer the questions.

Ducks have wide feet. They use them to swim. Ducks move their feet under water.

1. Why do ducks move their feet under water?

_____

_____

_____

2. A duck's feet are

_____

_____

_____

3. Color the duck's feet orange.

Name: _____

Ducks In The Park

Directions: Read about ducks in the park. Then answer the questions.

Have you ever been to a park? Did you see baby ducks? Baby ducks can swim and walk. They can find their own food. Can you?

1. The main idea is:

   You can go to a park.

   Baby ducks can do many things.

2. Name 3 things baby ducks can do.

   1) _____ 2) _____

   3) _____

3. What would you name a baby duck?

   _____

   _____

Name: _____

Review

Directions: Read about goats. Then follow the instructions.

Goats make good pets. Like cows, goats give milk. Cows eat grass. Goats eat grass, too.

Here is how to make a goat your pet: 3 days after it is born, take it from its mother. Then feed it from a bottle. Hold it and pet it. The goat will think you are its mother.

1. What do both goats and cows eat?

_____

_____

2. The main idea is:

      Goats make good pets.

      Goats and cows eat grass.

3. Tell how to make a pet of your goat.

1) Take it from its mother when it is 3 days old.

_____

2) _____

_____

3) _____

_____

4. Why will the goat think you are its mother?

_____

_____

_____

Name: _____

Outside Games/Inside Games

Directions: Read about games. Then color the games you can play inside. Circle the things for outside games.

   Some games are outside games. Some games are inside games. Outside games are active. Inside games are quiet. Which do you like best?

Name: _____

Ann And Lee Jump Rope

Directions: Read about jumping rope. Then answer the questions.

Ann and Lee like to jump rope. Ann likes to jump rope alone. Lee likes to have 2 people turn the rope for him. Ann and Lee can jump slow. They can also jump fast.

1. Name 1 more way to jump rope:

1) Have 2 people turn the rope.

_____

2) _____

_____

2. Name 2 speeds for jumping rope:

_____ _____

_____ _____

3. Do you like to jump rope?

_____

_____

_____

Name: _____

Oops! For Lee And Ann

Directions: Look at the pictures on the left. On the right, show and tell what you predict will happen next.

_____
_____
_____
_____
_____
_____
_____
_____
_____

_____
_____
_____
_____
_____
_____
_____
_____

_____
_____
_____
_____
_____
_____
_____
_____

Name: _____

Yo-Yos

Directions: Read about yo-yos. Then answer the questions.

Yo-yo is a funny word. It means "come-come." Why? Move the yo-yo away from you on its string. It will always come back!

1. The main idea is:

    You can move a yo-yo on a string.

    Yo-yo means "come-come" because it always comes back.

2. A yo-yo moves:

    slowly.

    on a string.

3. Color the yo-yo.

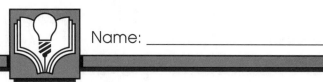

Name: _____

A Yo-Yo Trick

Directions: Read about the yo-yo trick. Then draw a line to match the directions with the correct pictures. Number the steps in the directions.

Wind up the yo-yo string. Hold the yo-yo in your hand. Now, hold your palm up. Throw the yo-yo downward on the string. Hold your palm down. Now swing the yo-yo forward. Make it "walk." This yo-yo trick is called "walk the dog."

_____Swing the yo-yo forward and make it "walk."

_____Hold your palm up and drop the yo-yo.

_____Turn your palm down as the yo-yo reaches the ground.

Name: _____

Ann And Lee Like Art

Directions: Read about Ann and Lee. Then answer the questions.

Ann and Lee like art. They both like to color. They both like to draw. They both like to paint. Do you like art?

1. Name 3 things Ann and Lee like about art.

1) _____

2) _____

3) _____

2. Draw a line from the words that tell about the pictures.

color

draw

paint

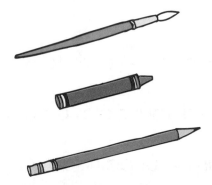

Name: _____

Ann And Lee Have Fun

Directions: Read about Ann and Lee. Then tell how they are the same and different.

Ann and Lee like to play ball. They like to jump rope. Lee likes to play a card game called "Old Maid." Ann likes to play a card game called "Go Fish." What do you do to have fun?

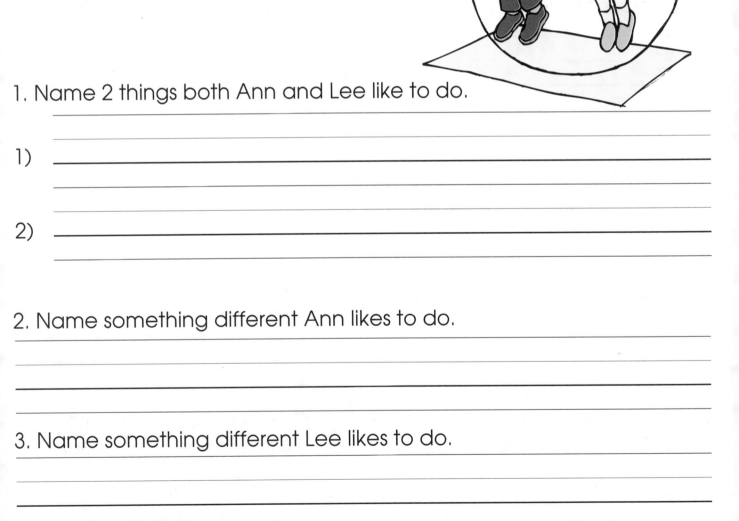

1. Name 2 things both Ann and Lee like to do.

1) _____

_____

2) _____

_____

2. Name something different Ann likes to do.

_____

_____

3. Name something different Lee likes to do.

_____

_____

_____

Review

There are many ways to have fun. You can bounce a ball. You can play with a yo-yo. You can jump rope. You can play a card game called "Old Maid."

1. The main idea is:

 Jumping rope is fun.

 There are many ways to have fun.

2. List in order the ways to have fun:

1) Bounce a ball.

_____

2) _____ 3) _____

_____   _____

4) Play Old Maid.

3. A way these games are the same is:

 You use your hands to play them.

 Some are played inside.

4. Predict what games kids will play when it is rainy and cold.

_____   _____

_____   _____

_____   _____

5. Put an **I** beside indoor games. Put an **O** beside outdoor games. Put an **I/O** beside the thing you can play with indoors or outdoors.

_____ Bounce a ball.   _____ Play Old Maid.

_____ Jump rope.   _____ Play with a yo-yo.

How To Stop A Dog Fight

Directions: Read about how to stop a dog fight. Then answer the questions.

Sometimes dogs fight. They bark loud. They may bite. Do not try to pull apart fighting dogs. Turn on a hose and spray them with water. This will stop the fight.

1. Name something dogs may do if they are mad.

_____

_____

_____

_____

2. Why is it unwise to pull on dogs that are fighting?

_____

_____

_____

_____

3. Do you think dogs like to get wet? _____

_____

_____

Name: _____

Training A Dog

Directions: Read about how to train dogs. Then answer the questions.

A dog has a ball in his mouth. You want the ball. What should you do? Do not pull on the ball. Hold out something else for the dog. The dog will drop the ball to take it!

1. The main idea is:

   Always get a ball away from a dog.

   Offer the dog something else to get him to drop the ball.

2. What should you **not** do if you want the dog's ball?

   _____

   _____

   _____

3. What could you hold out for the dog to take?

   _____

   _____

   _____

Name: _____

How To Meet A Dog

Directions: Read about how to meet a dog. Then follow the instructions.

Do not try to pet a dog right away. First, let the dog sniff your hand. Do not move fast. Do not talk loud. Just let the dog sniff.

1. Predict what the dog will let you do if it likes you.

_____

_____

_____

2. What should you let the dog do?

_____

_____

_____

3. Name 3 things you should **not** do when you meet a dog.

_____

1) _____

_____

2) _____

_____

3) _____

_____

53

Name: _____

Ladybugs

Directions: Read about ladybugs. Then answer the questions.

Have you ever seen a ladybug? Ladybugs are red. They have black spots. They have six legs. Ladybugs are pretty!

1. What color are ladybugs?

_____
_____
_____

2. What color are their spots?

_____
_____
_____

3. How many legs do ladybugs have?

_____
_____
_____

Name: _____

How To Treat A Ladybug

Directions: Read how to treat ladybugs. Then follow the instructions.

Ladybugs are shy. If you see a ladybug, sit very still. Hold out your arm. Maybe the ladybug will fly to you. If it does, talk softly. Do not touch it. It will fly away when it is ready.

1. Give directions on how to treat a ladybug.
1) Sit very still.

2) _____

3) Talk softly!

4) _____

2. Ladybugs are red.
   They have black spots.
   Color the ladybug.

Name: _____

Snakes!

Directions: Read about snakes. Then answer the questions.

Here are some facts about snakes: A snake's skin is dry. Most snakes are shy. They will hide from you. Snakes eat mice and rats. They do not chew them up. Snakes' jaws drop open to swallow their food.

1. How does a snake's skin feel? _____

_____

_____

2. Most snakes are _____

_____

3. Name 2 things snakes eat.

1) _____   2) _____

_____

Name: _____

More About Snakes

Directions: Read more about snakes. Then answer the questions.

Unlike people, snakes have cold blood. They like to be warm. They hunt for food when it is warm. They lie in the sun. When it is cold, snakes curl up into a ball.

1. Name 2 things snakes do when it is warm.

1) _____

_____

2) _____

_____

2. Why do you think snakes curl up when it is cold?

_____

_____

_____

3. People have: cold blood.

warm blood.

Name: _____

Review

Directions: Read about birds. Then answer the questions.

Birds use many things to make their nests. They use twigs. They use moss. Birds will even use hair and yarn. You can help birds make a nest. Here's how: Cut up some yarn. Ask a grown-up to trim your hair. Then put the yarn and hair outdoors.

1. The main idea is:

Birds use many things to make nests.

Cut your hair to help a bird.

2. Tell how to help a bird make a nest.

_____

1) _____

_____

2) _____

_____

3) Put the yarn and hair outdoors.

3. Why do you think birds like yarn and hair?

_____

_____

_____

4. Predict what birds will do with the yarn and hair.

_____

_____

_____

Name: _____

Shell Homes

Directions: Read about shells. Then answer the questions.

Shells are the homes of some animals. Snails live in shells on the land. Clams live in shells in the water. Clam shells open. Snail shells stay closed. All shells keep animals safe.

 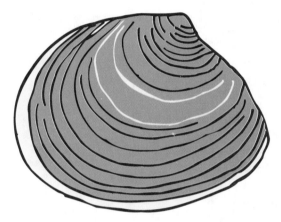

1. Snails live in shells on the

   water.

   land.

2. Clam shells are different from snail shells because

   they open.

   they stay closed.

3. Tell 1 way all shells are the same.

   _____

   _____

   _____

Name: _____

Sea Horses Look Strange!

Directions: Read about sea horses. Then answer the questions.

Sea horses are fish, not horses. A sea horse's head looks like a horse's head. It has a tail like a monkey's tail. A sea horse looks very strange!

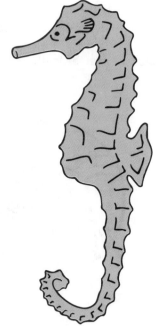

1. A sea horse is a kind of

   horse.

   monkey.

   fish.

2. What does a sea horse's head look like?

   _____

   _____

   _____

3. Name 2 things that make a sea horse look strange.

   _____

   1) _____

   _____

   2) _____

   _____

Name: _____

More About Sea Horses

Directions: Read more about sea horses. Then answer the questions.

A father sea horse helps the mother. He has a small sack or pouch on the front of his body. The mother sea horse lays the eggs. She does not keep them. She gives the eggs to the father.

1. What does the mother sea horse do with her eggs?

_____

_____

_____

2. Where does the father sea horse put the eggs?

_____

_____

_____

3. Sea horses can change color. Color the sea horses any color you want.

Singing Whales

Directions: Read about singing whales. Answer the questions.

Some whales can sing! We cannot understand the words. But we can hear the tune of the humpback whale. Each season, humpback whales sing a different song.

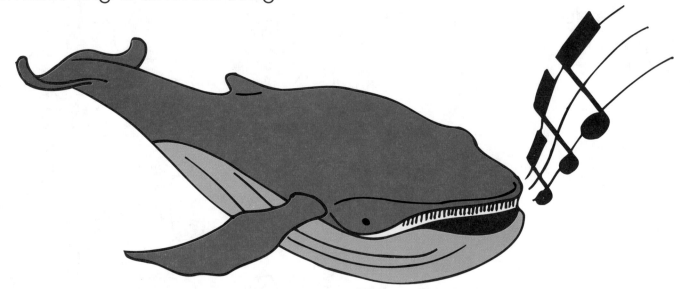

1. The main idea is:

    All whales can sing.

    Some whales can sing.

2. Name the kind of whale that sings.

    _____

    _____

    _____

3. How many different songs does the humpback sing each year?

    1   2   3   4

Name: _____

Sleeping Whales

Directions: Read more about whales. Then answer the questions.

Whales do not sleep like we do. They take many short naps. Like us, whales breathe air. But whales live in very cold water. Whales have fat that keeps them warm.

1. How are whales and people the same?
_____
_____
_____

2. Tell 2 ways whales and people are different.
_____

1) _____
_____

2) _____
_____

3) Whales have fat that keeps them warm.

Name: _____

Review

Directions: Read about whales and sea horses. Then answer the questions.

Whales and sea horses both live in the ocean. Sea horses grow to be about 6 inches long. Whales can grow to be 100 feet long. Sea horses swim with their heads up and tails down. Whales swim on their bellies.

1. The main idea is:

Whales and sea horses are alike.

Whales and sea horses are very different.

2. Tell 1 way whales and sea horses are the same.

_____

_____

_____

3. Tell 2 ways whales and sea horses are different.

1) _____

_____

2) _____

_____

4. Predict whether whales would be afraid of sea horses.

                    Yes   No

Three of Everything

Make lists of things in your classroom or your home.
Do not worry about spelling. Just do your best.

List 3 things used for cooking.

_____

_____

_____

List 3 things you use every day.

_____

_____

_____

List 3 things that use electricity.

_____

_____

_____

List 3 things you sit on.

_____

_____

_____

List 3 things you can open.

_____

_____

_____

Developing sight vocabulary

Word Pictures

You can write a word to look like its meaning.
Look at these words.

| little 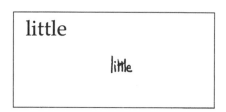 | mad  | fat 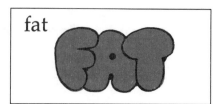 |

Now it is your turn.
Read each word.
Write or draw the word so it looks like its meaning.

| high | round |
| silly | fall |

Developing sight vocabulary

Word Hunt

Make the words below into compound words.
Use words from the box to make the
compound words.
Then hunt for the compound words
in the Word Hunt.
The words go across. The words go up and down.
Circle each compound word you find.

fish	yard	ball
town	box	top
paper	book	walk
chair	tub	shine

base __ball_____   down _____   news_____

lunch_____   note_____   arm _____

side_____   sun _____   hill _____

gold_____   back_____   bath _____

Word Hunt

m	n	s	u	n	s	h	i	n	e	h
g	o	l	d	f	i	s	h	p	b	i
f	t	m	w	q	r	i	l	y	a	l
p	e	n	l	v	c	d	w	b	t	l
b	b	e	u	v	x	e	m	a	h	t
d	o	w	n	t	o	w	n	s	t	o
z	o	s	c	z	s	a	p	e	u	p
g	k	p	h	i	j	l	t	b	b	x
o	v	a	b	a	c	k	y	a	r	d
k	l	p	o	e	i	u	h	l	j	m
y	m	e	x	b	r	a	y	l	h	z
f	a	r	m	c	h	a	i	r	t	o

Forming compound words

Line Designs

Draw a line from the words to the contraction
that means the same.
When you finish, you will have some nice pictures
in the middle.

is not •   • he'll

we are •   • we're

he will •   • isn't

I will •   • didn't

have not •   • that's

they will •   • couldn't

could not •   • they'll

that is •   • haven't

did not •   • I'll

she is •   • you're

can not •   • can't

you are •   • she's

Identifying contractions

Make a Cat

Do this with a grown-up.
If you want to, make a whole family of cats.

1. Start with a square piece of paper.

2. Fold the square to make a triangle.

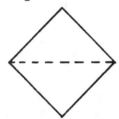

3. Fold the top point of the triangle down and forward.

4. Fold the bottom points up and forward.

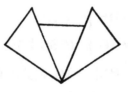

5. Turn the paper around and draw a cat face.

What's the Game?

Have a grown-up read these rules to you.

You need 2 players.
You play on a board that is covered with red and black squares.
One player uses round red pieces.
The other player uses round black pieces.
The pieces slide around the board.
Pieces can also jump.
Red pieces capture black pieces by jumping over them.
Black pieces capture red pieces by jumping over them.
You try to capture all the other player's pieces.

Can you name the game?

What is the game? _____

Here are the names of some games.

     baseball   basketball   soccer

     tic-tac-toe   hopscotch   chess

Choose one of the games.
Tell your grown-up how to play.
Do not say the name of the game.
Have your grown-up try to guess the name of the game.
Then let your grown-up explain a game.
You guess the name of the game.

My game was _____.

What game did your grown-up guess? _____

My grown-up's game was _____.

What game did you guess? _____

Drawing conclusions

What Next?

Read this story with a grown-up.

    Lola was running up the school steps. She was in a hurry. She had the lead part in her school play, and the show was about to start. Suddenly Lola tripped. She twisted her foot. It hurt a lot. Lola tried to walk, but her foot hurt too much.

What will happen next?
Write your idea.

_____

_____

_____

_____

_____

What does your grown-up think will happen next?
Let your grown-up write his or her idea.

_____

_____

_____

_____

_____

Predicting outcomes   71

Before, During, After

Ask a grown-up to guess what you did today.
Your grown-up must guess something you did
before lunch, during lunch, and after lunch.
Have your grown-up write the guesses here.

Before lunch _____

During lunch _____

After lunch _____

Were your grown-up's guesses right?

Before lunch _____ During lunch _____ After lunch_____

Now it is your turn.
Guess what your grown-up did before lunch,
during lunch, and after lunch.
Write your guesses here.

Before lunch _____

_____

During lunch _____

_____

After lunch _____

_____

Were your guesses right?

Before lunch_____ During lunch _____ After lunch_____

ANSWER KEY

MASTER COMPREHENSION
2

A Game For Cats

Directions: Read about what cats like. Then follow the instructions.

Cats like to play with paper bags. Pull a paper bag open. Take everything out. Now lay it on its side.

1. Put the pictures in 1, 2, 3 order.
2. In 4, draw what you think the cat will do.

picture varies

5

Pretty Parrots

Directions: Read about parrots. Then follow the instructions.

Big parrots are pretty. Their feet each have four toes. Two toes are in front. Two toes are in back. Parrots use their feet to climb. They use them to hold food.

1. A parrot's foot has   4 toes / 2 toes

2. Name 2 things a parrot does with his feet.
1) climb   2) hold food

3. Color the parrot.

6

Parrot Art

Directions: Draw the parts that are missing on each parrot.

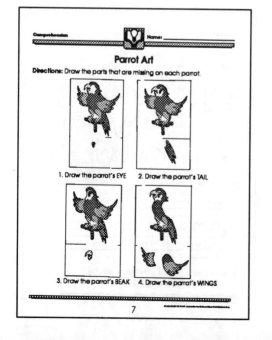

1. Draw the parrot's EYE   2. Draw the parrot's TAIL

3. Draw the parrot's BEAK   4. Draw the parrot's WINGS

7

Dirty Dogs

Directions: Read about dogs. Then follow the instructions.

Like people, dogs get dirty. Some dogs get a bath once a month. Baby soap is a good soap for cleaning dogs. Fill a tub with warm water. Get someone to hold the dog still in the tub. Then wash the dog fast.

1. How often do some dogs get a bath?
once a month

2. What is a good soap to use on dogs?
baby soap

3. Do you think most dogs like to take baths?
no

8

Dog-gone!

Directions: Read the story. Then follow the instructions.

Ben and Ann were washing Spot. His fur was wet. Their hands were wet. Spot did NOT like to be wet. Ben dropped the soap. Ann picked it up and let go of Spot. Uh-oh!

1. Tell what happened next.
Spot jumped out of the tub.

2. Draw what happened next.

9

Review

Directions: Read about how to move the goldfish. Then follow the instructions.

Here is how to move a goldfish into a new bowl:
1. Fill the new bowl with fresh water. 2. Put the net under the fish and lift it from the old bowl. 3. Turn the net upside down. Close the net over your hand so the fish can't jump out. 4. Turn the net upside down over the fresh bowl of water. Let the fish drop in.

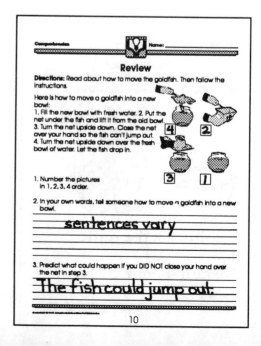

1. Number the pictures in 1, 2, 3, 4 order.

2. In your own words, tell someone how to move a goldfish into a new bowl.
sentences vary

3. Predict what could happen if you DID NOT close your hand over the net in step 3.
The fish could jump out.

10

Find The Puppets

Directions: Read about puppets. Then follow the instructions.

There are many kinds of puppets. Some puppets fit on your hand. Some puppets fit on your fingers. Some puppets are moved by strings.

Find and color the 3 puppets on this page. What kind of puppets did you find?

1. **hand**   2. **finger**   3. **string**

11

New Cards From Old

Directions: Read about making cards. Then answer the questions.

Did you ever get a card? Do you still have it? You can use it to make a new card. Then you can give the new card away.

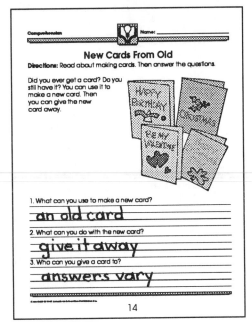

1. What can you use to make a new card?

an old card

2. What can you do with the new card?

give it away

3. Who can you give a card to?

answers vary

14

Paper Sack Puppets

Directions: Read about paper sack puppets. Then follow the instructions.

It is easy to make a hand puppet. You need a small sack. You need colored paper. You need glue. You need scissors. Are you ready?

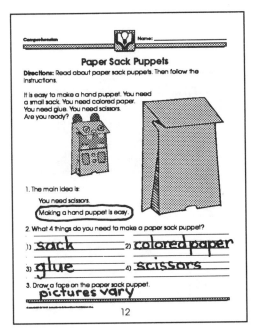

1. The main idea is:

     You need scissors.

     (Making a hand puppet is easy.)

2. What 4 things do you need to make a paper sack puppet?

1) **sack**   2) **colored paper**

3) **glue**   4) **scissors**

3. Draw a face on the paper sack puppet.

pictures vary

12

Making A Card

Directions: Read about how to make a card. Then follow the instructions.

You will need scissors and glue. Find some colored paper. First, look at all your old cards. Then, cut out what you like. Now, fold the colored paper in half. Glue onto the front what you have cut out. Write your name inside.

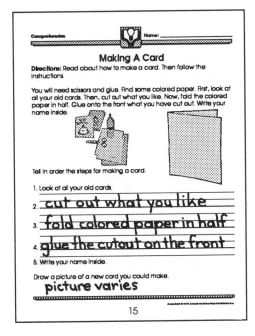

Tell in order the steps for making a card.

1. Look at all your old cards.

2. **cut out what you like**

3. **fold colored paper in half**

4. **glue the cutout on the front**

5. Write your name inside.

Draw a picture of a new card you could make.

picture varies

15

Make A Paper Sack Puppet

Directions: Read how to make a paper sack puppet. Then follow the instructions.

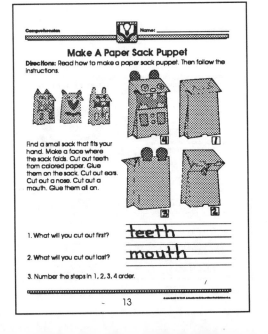

Find a small sack that fits your hand. Make a face where the sack folds. Cut out teeth from colored paper. Glue them on the sack. Cut out ears. Cut out a nose. Cut out a mouth. Glue them all on.

1. What will you cut out first?   **teeth**

2. What will you cut out last?   **mouth**

3. Number the steps in 1, 2, 3, 4 order.

13

Types Of Tops

Directions: Read about tops. Then answer the questions.

Tops come in all sizes. Some tops are made of wood. Some tops are made of tin. All tops do the same thing. They spin! Do you have a top?

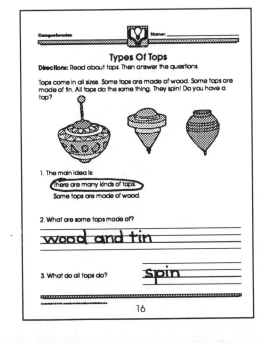

1. The main idea is:

     (There are many kinds of tops.)

     Some tops are made of wood.

2. What are some tops made of?

wood and tin

3. What do all tops do?   **spin**

16

Tip Top

Directions: Read about the girl's top. Then follow the instructions.

A girl gets a new top. She wants it put up where it is safe. She asks her dad to put it up high. Where can her dad put it?

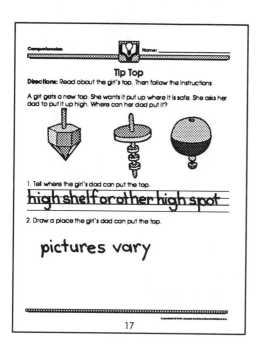

1. Tell where the girl's dad can put the top.

high shelf or other high spot

2. Draw a place the girl's dad can put the top.

pictures vary

17

Review

Directions: Read about making clay. Then follow the instructions.

It is fun to work with clay. Here is what you need to make it:
1 cup salt   2 cups flour   3/4 cup water

Mix the salt and flour. Then add the water.
Do NOT eat the clay. It tastes bad.
Use your hands to mix and mix.
Now roll it out. What can you make?

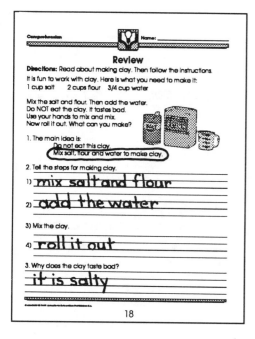

1. The main idea is:
   Do not eat this clay.
   (Mix salt, flour and water to make clay.)

2. Tell the steps for making clay.

1) **mix salt and flour**

2) **add the water**

3) Mix the clay.

4) **roll it out**

3. Why does the clay taste bad?

it is salty

18

Using Tools

Directions: Read about art tools. Then color only the art tools.

You need tools for art. To cut, you need scissors. To draw, you need a pencil. To color, you need a crayon. To paint, you need a brush.

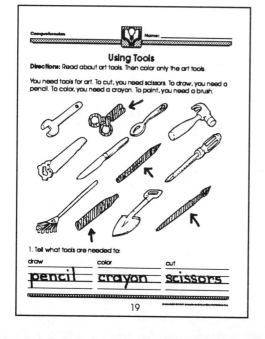

1. Tell what tools are needed to:

draw	color	cut
pencil	**crayon**	**scissors**

19

About Ant Farms

Directions: Read about ant farms. Then answer the questions.

Ant farms are sold at toy stores and pet stores. Ant farms come in a flat frame. The frame has glass on each side. Inside the glass is sand. The ants live in the sand.

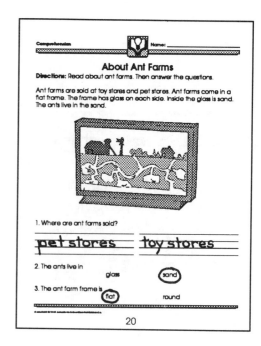

1. Where are ant farms sold?

pet stores   **toy stores**

2. The ants live in

glass   (sand)

3. The ant farm frame is

(flat)   round

20

Down On The Ant Farm

Directions: Read about ants. Then follow the instructions.

Ants are busy on the farm. They dig in the sand. They make roads in the sand. They look for food in the sand. When an ant dies, other ants bury it.

1. Where do you think ants are buried?

in the sand

2. Is it fair to say ants are lazy?

no

3. Write a word that tells about ants.

busy

21

Just Junk?

Directions: Read about junk. Then follow the instructions.

Do you save old crayons? Do you save old buttons or cards? Some kids call these things junk. They throw them out. Some kids save these things. They put them in a box. What do you do?

The main idea is:
   Everyone has junk.
   (People have different ideas about what junk is.)

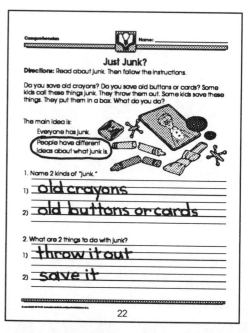

1. Name 2 kinds of "junk."

1) **old crayons**

2) **old buttons or cards**

2. What are 2 things to do with junk?

1) **throw it out**

2) **save it**

22

76

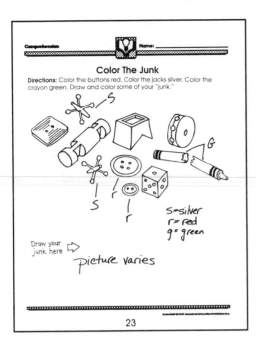

Color The Junk

Directions: Color the buttons red. Color the jacks silver. Color the crayon green. Draw and color some of your "junk."

S=silver
r=red
g=green

Draw your junk here ➡ *picture varies*

23

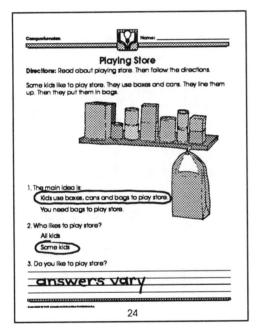

Playing Store

Directions: Read about playing store. Then follow the directions.

Some kids like to play store. They use boxes and cans. They line them up. Then they put them in bags.

1. The main idea is:
   (Kids use boxes, cans and bags to play store.)
   You need bags to play store.

2. Who likes to play store?
   All kids
   (Some kids)

3. Do you like to play store?
   answers vary

24

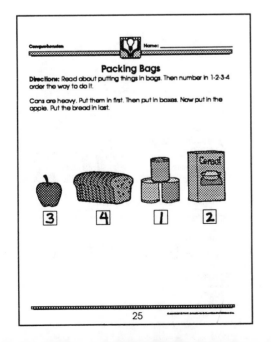

Packing Bags

Directions: Read about putting things in bags. Then number in 1-2-3-4 order the way to do it.

Cans are heavy. Put them in first. Then put in boxes. Now put in the apple. Put the bread in last.

[3] [4] [1] [2]

25

Review

Directions: Read the story. Then answer the questions.

Ann has many books. Some of Ann's books are about dogs. Some are about games. Some are about plants. Ann wants a pet. She reads about it in one of her books.

1. The main idea is:
   (Ann learns things from books.)
   Ann likes games.

2. Would you classify Ann as:
   (A person who likes to read.)
   A person who does not like to read.

3. What kind of pet does Ann want?
   a dog

4. Give directions on 1 way to learn about pets.
   read about pets in books

26

Do You Like Jokes?

Directions: Read about jokes. Then follow the instructions.

Most kids like jokes. Some jokes are long. Some jokes are short. Good jokes are funny. Do you know a funny joke?

1. The main idea is:
   (There are many kinds of jokes.)
   Some jokes are short.

2. What did the rug say to the floor?
   I've got you covered.

27

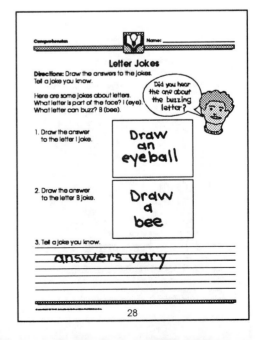

Letter Jokes

Directions: Draw the answers to the jokes. Tell a joke you know.

Here are some jokes about letters. What letter is part of the face? I (eye). What letter can buzz? B (bee).

Did you hear the one about the buzzing letter?

1. Draw the answer to the letter I joke.
   Draw an eyeball

2. Draw the answer to the letter B joke.
   Draw a bee

3. Tell a joke you know.
   answers vary

28

Color And Number Jokes

Directions: Read about jokes. Then answer the questions.

Here are more jokes! Do you know what color is loud? Do you know what number is not hungry?

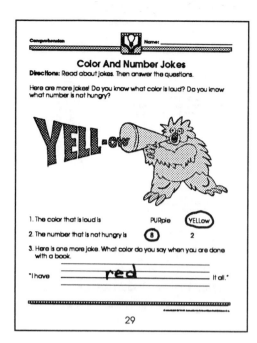

1. The color that is loud is   PURple   (YELLow)

2. The number that is not hungry is   (8)   2

3. Here is one more joke. What color do you say when you are done with a book.

"I have ___red___ it all."

29

A Rainy Day

Directions: Read the story. Circle the things Lee needs to stay dry.

It is raining. Lee wants to play outdoors. What should he wear to stay dry? What should he carry to stay dry?

32

A Winter Story

Directions: Read the story. Then answer the questions.

It is cold in winter. Snow falls. Water freezes. Most kids like to play outdoors. Some kids make a snowman. Some kids skate. What do you do in winter?

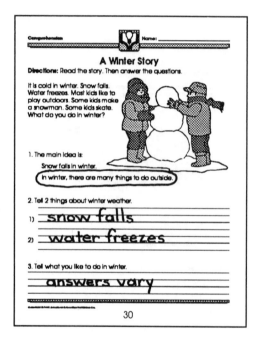

1. The main idea is:

   Snow falls in winter.

   (In winter, there are many things to do outside.)

2. Tell 2 things about winter weather.

1) ___snow falls___

2) ___water freezes___

3. Tell what you like to do in winter.

___answers vary___

30

Baking A Cake

Directions: Read the story. Then give directions on how to bake a cake.

Ann, Lee and Dad will bake a cake. Dad turns on the oven. Ann opens the cake mix. Lee adds the eggs. Dad pours in the water. Ann stirs it. Lee pours the batter into a cake pan. Dad puts it in the oven.

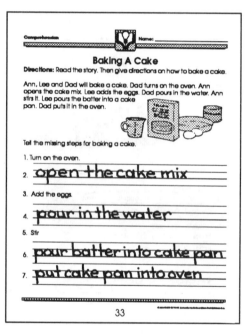

Tell the missing steps for baking a cake.

1. Turn on the oven.

2. ___open the cake mix___

3. Add the eggs.

4. ___pour in the water___

5. Stir

6. ___pour batter into cake pan___

7. ___put cake pan into oven___

33

Making A Snowman

Directions: Read the story. Then follow the instructions.

It is fun to make a snowman. First, find things for the snowman's eyes and nose. Dress warmly. Then go outdoors. Roll a big snowball. Then roll another to put on top of it. Now roll a small snowball for the head. Put on the snowman's face.

1. Name 2 things to do before going outdoors.

1) ___find thing for snowmans eyes/nose___

2) ___dress warmly___

2. Number the steps in the right order.

31

Review

Directions: Read the story. Then follow the instructions.

The cake is done. It is taken from the oven. Ann and Lee want to frost it. "I want to use this white frosting," says Ann. "I want to use my red frosting," says Lee. "We will use both your ideas," says Dad. "We will have pink frosting."

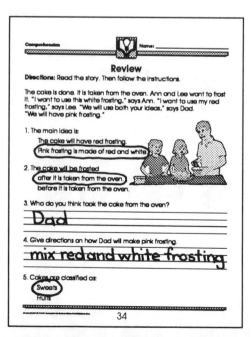

1. The main idea is:

   The cake will have red frosting.

   (Pink frosting is made of red and white.)

2. The cake will be frosted

   (after it is taken from the oven.)

   before it is taken from the oven.

3. Who do you think took the cake from the oven?

___Dad___

4. Give directions on how Dad will make pink frosting.

___mix red and white frosting___

5. Cakes are classified as:

   (Sweets)

   Fruits

34

Bluebirds And Parrots

Directions: Read about parrots and bluebirds. Tell how they are the same and different.

Bluebirds and parrots are both birds. Bluebirds and parrots can fly. They both have beaks. Parrots can live inside in a cage. Bluebirds must live outdoors.

1. Tell 2 ways bluebirds and parrots are the same.

1) **they are both birds**

2) **they both fly or have beaks**

2. Tell 1 way these birds are different.

Bluebirds must live

outdoors

Parrots can live

inside a cage

35

Fish

Directions: Read about fish. Then follow the instructions.

Some fish live in warm water. Some fish live in cold water. Some fish live in lakes. Some fish live in oceans. There are 20,000 kinds of fish!

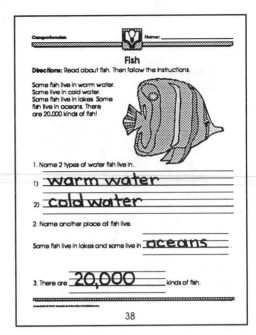

1. Name 2 types of water fish live in.

1) **warm water**

2) **cold water**

2. Name another place all fish live.

Some fish live in lakes and some live in **oceans**

3. There are **20,000** kinds of fish.

38

Tigers

Directions: Read the story. Follow the instructions.

Tigers grow to be big! Some grow to be 10 feet long. Baby tigers are called cubs. They are small.

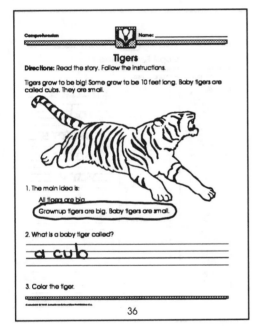

1. The main idea is:

   All tigers are big

   (Grownup tigers are big. Baby tigers are small.)

2. What is a baby tiger called?

   a cub

3. Color the tiger.

36

Fish Come In Many Colors

Directions: Read about the color of fish. Then tell the colors and color the fish.

All fish live in water. Fish that live at the top are blue, green or black. Fish that live down deep are silver or red. The colors make it hard to see the fish.

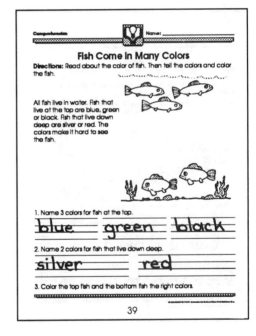

1. Name 3 colors for fish at the top.

   blue   **green**   **black**

2. Name 2 colors for fish that live down deep.

   silver   **red**

3. Color the top fish and the bottom fish the right colors.

39

Cats And Tigers

Directions: Read about cats and tigers. Tell how they are the same and different.

Tigers are a kind of cat. Pet cats and tigers both have fur. Pet cats are small and tame. Tigers are large and wild.

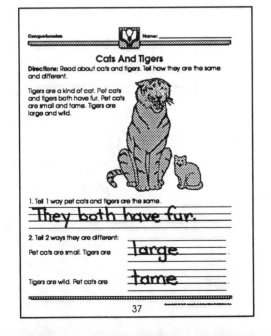

1. Tell 1 way pet cats and tigers are the same.

They both have fur.

2. Tell 2 ways they are different:

Pet cats are small. Tigers are **large**

Tigers are wild. Pet cats are **tame**

Bluebirds And Parrots

37

Just Ducky

Directions: Read about ducks. Then answer the questions.

Ducks have wide feet. They use them to swim. Ducks move their feet under water.

1. Why do ducks move their feet under water?

   to swim

2. A duck's feet are

   wide

3. Color the duck's feet orange.

40

79

Ducks In The Park

Directions: Read about ducks in the park. Then answer the questions.

Have you ever been to a park? Did you see baby ducks? Baby ducks can swim and walk. They can find their own food. Can you?

1. The main idea is:

    You can go to a park.

    (Baby ducks can do many things.)

2. Name 3 things baby ducks can do.

1) **swim**   2) **walk**

3) **find their own food**

3. What would you name a baby duck?

    answers vary

41

Ann And Lee Jump Rope

Directions: Read about jumping rope. Then answer the questions.

Ann and Lee like to jump rope. Ann likes to jump rope alone. Lee likes to have 2 people turn the rope for him. Ann and Lee can jump slow. They can also jump fast.

1. Name 1 more way to jump rope:

1) Have 2 people turn the rope.

2) **jump alone**

2. Name 2 speeds for jumping rope:

slow   **fast**

3. Do you like to jump rope?

    answers vary

44

Review

Directions: Read about goats. Then follow the instructions.

Goats make good pets. Like cows, goats give milk. Cows eat grass. Goats eat grass too.

Here is how to make a goat your pet: 3 days after it is born, take it from its mother. Then feed it from a bottle. Hold it and pet it. The goat will think you are its mother!

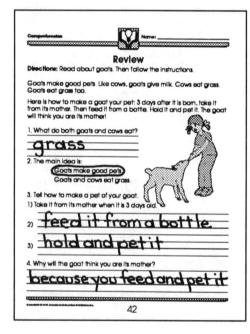

1. What do both goats and cows eat?

grass

2. The main idea is:

    (Goats make good pets.)

    Goats and cows eat grass.

3. Tell how to make a pet of your goat.

1) Take it from its mother when it is 3 days old.

2) **feed it from a bottle**

3) **hold and pet it**

4. Why will the goat think you are its mother?

because you feed and pet it

42

Oops! For Lee And Ann

Directions: Look at the pictures on the left. On the right, show and tell what you predict will happen next.

pictures and answers will vary

45

Outside Games/Inside Games

Directions: Read about games. Then color the games you can play inside. Circle the things for outside games.

Some games are outside games. Some games are inside games. Outside games are active. Inside games are quiet. Which do you like best?

43

Yo-Yos

Directions: Read about yo-yos. Then answer the questions.

Yo-yo is a funny word. It means "come-come." Why? Move the yo-yo away from you on its string. It will always come back!

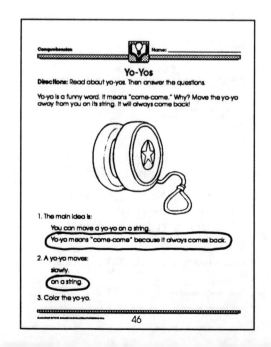

1. The main idea is:

    You can move a yo-yo on a string.

    (Yo-yo means "come-come" because it always comes back.)

2. A yo-yo moves:

    slowly.

    (on a string.)

3. Color the yo-yo.

46

A Yo-Yo Trick

Directions: Read about the yo-yo trick. Then draw a line to match the directions with the correct pictures. Number the steps in the directions.

Wind up the yo-yo string. Hold the yo-yo in your hand. Now, hold your palm up. Throw the yo-yo downward on the string. Hold your palm down. Now swing the yo-yo forward. Make it "walk." This yo-yo trick is called "walk the dog."

_3_ Swing the yo-yo forward and make it "walk."

_1_ Hold your palm up and drop the yo-yo.

_2_ Turn your palm down as the yo-yo reaches the ground.

47

Review

There are many ways to have fun. You can bounce a ball. You can play with a yo-yo. You can jump a rope. You can play a card game called Old Maid.

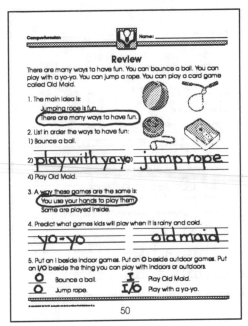

1. The main idea is:
   Jumping rope is fun.
   (There are many ways to have fun.)

2. List in order the ways to have fun:
   1) Bounce a ball.
   2) _play with yo-yo_   _jump rope_
   4) Play Old Maid.

3. A way these games are the same is:
   (You use your hands to play them)
   Some are played inside.

4. Predict what games kids will play when it is rainy and cold.
   _yo-yo_   _old maid_

5. Put an I beside indoor games. Put an O beside outdoor games. Put an I/O beside the thing you can play with indoors or outdoors.
   _O_ Bounce a ball.   _I/O_ Play Old Maid.
   _O_ Jump rope.   _I/O_ Play with a yo-yo.

50

Ann And Lee Like Art

Directions: Read about Ann and Lee. Then answer the questions.

Ann and Lee like art. They both like to color. They both like to draw. They both like to paint. Do you like art?

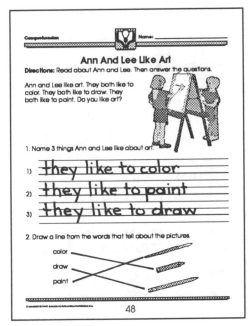

1. Name 3 things Ann and Lee like about art.

1) _they like to color_

2) _they like to paint_

3) _they like to draw_

2. Draw a line from the words that tell about the pictures.

color
draw
paint

48

How To Stop A Dog Fight

Directions: Read about how to stop a dog fight. Then answer the questions.

Sometimes dogs fight. They bark loud. They may bite. Do not try to pull apart fighting dogs. Turn on a hose and spray them with water. This will stop the fight.

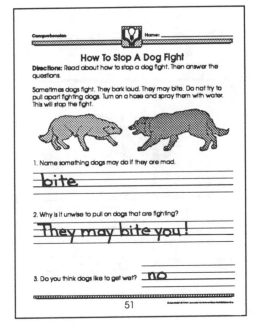

1. Name something dogs may do if they are mad.

bite

2. Why is it unwise to pull on dogs that are fighting?

They may bite you!

3. Do you think dogs like to get wet? _no_

51

Ann And Lee Have Fun

Directions: Read about Ann and Lee. Then tell how they are the same and different.

Ann and Lee like to play ball. They like to jump rope. Lee likes to play a card game called "Old Maid." Ann likes to play a card game called "Go Fish." What do you do to have fun?

1. Name 2 things both Ann and Lee like to do.

1) _play ball_

2) _jump rope_

2. Name something different Ann likes to do.

play "Go Fish"

3. Name something different Lee likes to do.

play "Old Maid"

49

Training A Dog

Directions: Read about how to train dogs. Then answer the questions.

A dog has a ball in his mouth. You want the ball. What should you do? Do not pull on the ball. Hold out something else for the dog. The dog will drop the ball to take it!

1. The main idea is:
   Always get a ball away from a dog.
   (Offer the dog something else to get him to drop the ball.)

2. What should you not do if you want the dog's ball?

pull on the ball

3. What could you hold out for the dog to take?

a stick, treat, etc.

How To Meet A Dog

Directions: Read about how to meet a dog. Then follow the instructions.

Do not try to pet a dog right away.
First let the dog sniff your hand.
Do not move fast. Do not talk loud.
Just let the dog sniff.

1. Predict what the dog will let you do if it likes you.

pet it

2. What should you let the dog do?

sniff your hand

3. Name 3 things you should **not** do when you meet a dog.

1) _pet it_
2) _move fast_
3) _talk loud_

53

Snakes!

Directions: Read about snakes. Then answer the questions.

Here are some facts about snakes: A snake's skin is dry. Most snakes are shy. They will hide from you. Snakes eat mice and rats. They do not chew them up. Snakes' jaws drop open to swallow their food.

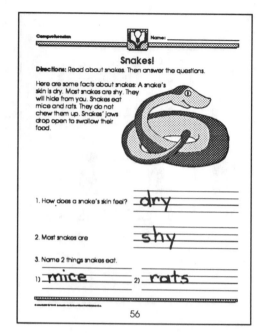

1. How does a snake's skin feel? _dry_

2. Most snakes are _shy_

3. Name 2 things snakes eat.

1) _mice_ 2) _rats_

56

Ladybugs

Directions: Read about ladybugs. Then answer the questions.

Have you ever seen a ladybug? Ladybugs are red. They have black spots. They have 6 legs. Ladybugs are pretty!

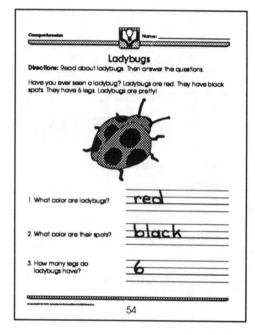

1. What color are ladybugs? _red_

2. What color are their spots? _black_

3. How many legs do ladybugs have? _6_

54

More About Snakes

Directions: Read more about snakes. Then answer the questions.

Unlike people, snakes have cold blood. They like to be warm. They hunt food when it is warm. They lie in the sun. When it is cold, snakes curl up into a ball.

1. Name 2 things snakes do when it is warm.

1) _hunt food_
2) _lie in the sun_

2. Why do you think snakes curl up when it is cold?

to keep warm

3. People have: cold blood
(warm blood)

57

How To Treat A Ladybug

Directions: Read how to treat ladybugs. Then follow the instructions.

Ladybugs are shy. If you see a ladybug, sit very still. Hold out your arm. Maybe the ladybug will fly to you. If it does, talk softly. Do not touch it. It will fly away when it is ready.

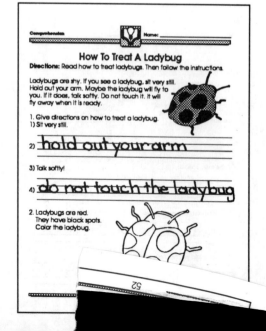

1. Give directions on how to treat a ladybug.
1) Sit very still.

2) _hold out your arm_

3) Talk softly!

4) _do not touch the ladybug_

2. Ladybugs are red.
   They have black spots.
   Color the ladybug.

52

Review

Directions: Read about birds. Then answer the questions.

Birds use many things to make their nests. They use twigs. They use moss. Birds will even use hair and yarn. You can help birds make a nest. Here's how: Cut up some yarn. Ask a grownup to trim your hair. Then put the yarn and hair outdoors.

1. The main idea is:
(Birds use many things to make nests)
   Cut your hair to help a bird.

2. Tell how to help a bird make a nest.

1) _cut up some yarn_
2) _ask a grownup to trim hair_

3) Put the yarn and hair outdoors.

3. Why do you think birds like yarn and hair?

they are soft

4. Predict what birds will do with the yarn and hair.

use them to make a nest

58

Shell Homes

Directions: Read about shells. Then answer the questions.

Shells are the homes of some animals. Snails live in shells on the land. Clams live in shells in the water. Clam shells open. Snail shells stay closed. All shells keep animals safe.

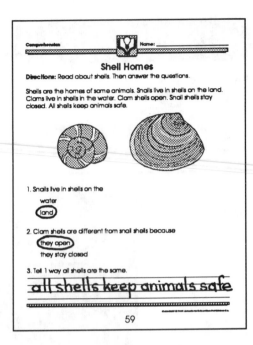

1. Snails live in shells on the

    water

    (land)

2. Clam shells are different from snail shells because

    (they open)

    they stay closed

3. Tell 1 way all shells are the same.

all shells keep animals safe

59

Sea Horses Look Strange!

Directions: Read about sea horses. Then answer the questions.

Sea horses are fish, not horses. A sea horse's head looks like a horse's head. It has a tail like a monkey's tail. A sea horse looks very strange!

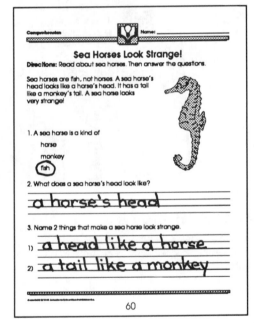

1. A sea horse is a kind of

    horse

    monkey

    (fish)

2. What does a sea horse's head look like?

a horse's head

3. Name 2 things that make a sea horse look strange.

1) *a head like a horse*

2) *a tail like a monkey*

60

More About Sea Horses

Directions: Read more about sea horses. Then answer the questions.

A father sea horse helps the mother. He has a small sack or pouch on the front of his body. The mother sea horse lays the eggs. She does not keep them. She gives the eggs to the father.

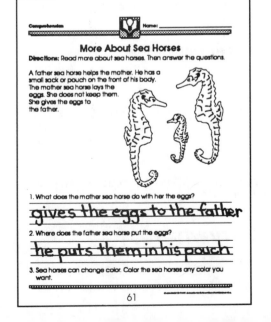

1. What does the mother sea horse do with her eggs?

gives the eggs to the father

2. Where does the father sea horse put the eggs?

he puts them in his pouch

3. Sea horses can change color. Color the sea horses any color you want.

61

Singing Whales

Directions: Read about singing whales. Answer the questions.

Some whales can sing! We cannot understand the words. But we can hear the tune of the humpback whale. Each season, humpback whales sing a different song.

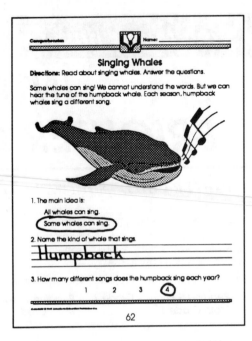

1. The main idea is:

    All whales can sing.

    (Some whales can sing.)

2. Name the kind of whale that sings.

Humpback

3. How many different songs does the humpback sing each year?

    1   2   3   (4)

62

Sleeping Whales

Directions: Read more about whales. Then answer the questions.

Whales do not sleep like we do. They take many short naps. Like us, whales breathe air. But whales live in very cold water. Whales have fat that keeps them warm.

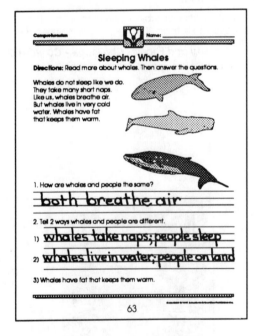

1. How are whales and people the same?

both breathe air

2. Tell 2 ways whales and people are different.

1) *whales take naps; people sleep*

2) *whales live in water; people on land*

3) Whales have fat that keeps them warm.

63

Review

Directions: Read about whales and sea horses. Then answer the questions.

Whales and sea horses both live in the ocean. Sea horses grow to be about 6 inches long. Whales can grow to be 100 feet long. Sea horses swim with their heads up and tails down. Whales swim on their bellies.

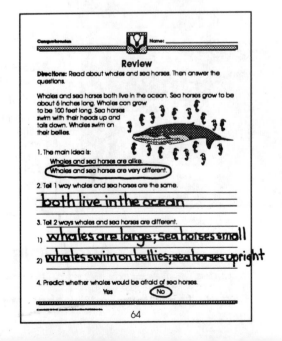

1. The main idea is:

    Whales and sea horses are alike.

    (Whales and sea horses are very different.)

2. Tell 1 way whales and sea horses are the same.

both live in the ocean

3. Tell 2 ways whales and sea horses are different.

1) *whales are large; sea horses small*

2) *whales swim on bellies; sea horses upright*

4. Predict whether whales would be afraid of sea horses.

    Yes   (No)

64

INTRODUCING
BRIGHTER CHILD™ SOFTWARE!

BRIGHTER CHILD ™ SOFTWARE for Windows

These colorful and exciting programs teach basic skills in an entertaining way. They are based on the best selling BRIGHTER CHILD™ workbooks, written and designed by experts who are also parents. Sound is included to facilitate learning, but it is not nesessary to run these programs. BRIGHTER CHILD™ software has received many outstanding reviews and awards. All Color! Easy to use!

The following programs are each sold separately in a 3.5 disk format.

Reading & Phonics Grade 1	Reading Grade 2	Reading Grade 3
Math Grade 1	Math Grade 2	Math Grade 3

CD-ROM Titles!

These new titles combine three grade levels of a subject on one CD-ROM! Each CD contains more than 80 different activities packed with colors and sound.

Reading and Phonics Challenge - CD-ROM Grades 1, 2, 3

Math Challenge - CD-ROM Grades 1, 2, 3

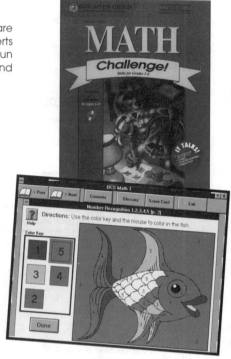

JIM HENSON'S MUPPET™/
BRIGHTER CHILD™ SOFTWARE for Windows™

Based on the best selling Muppet Press™/BRIGHTER CHILD™ Workbooks, these software programs for Windows are designed to teach basic concepts to children in preschool and kindergarten. Children will develop phonics skills and critical and creative thinking skills, and more! No reading is required with a sound card -- the directions are read aloud. The Muppet™ characters are universally known and loved and are recognized as having high educational value.

The following programs are each sold separately in a 3.5 disk format.
Each package contains:

- a program disk with more than 15 full color animated interactive lessons!
- sound is included which facilitates learning.
- Full-color workbook

Beginning Sounds: Phonics	Letters: Capital & Small
Same & Different	

CD-ROM Titles

Beginning Reading & Phonics- CD-ROM
This title combines three different MUPPET™/BRIGHTER CHILD™ Software programs -- Beginning Sounds: Phonics, Letters, and Same and Different -- all on one CD-ROM! This valuable software contains more than 50 different activities packed with color, sound, and interactive animation!

Reading & Phonics II- CD-ROM
Three Muppet™ Early Reading Programs on one CD-ROM. Includes *Sorting & Ordering, Thinking Skills,* and *Sound Patterns: More Phonics*

Available at stores everywhere.

OVERVIEW

ENRICHMENT READING is designed to provide children with practice in reading and to increase students' reading abilities. The program consists of six editions, one each for grades 1 through 6. The major areas of reading instruction--word skills, vocabulary, study skills, comprehension, and literary forms--are covered as appropriate at each level.

ENRICHMENT READING provides a wide range of activities that target a variety of skills in each instructional area. The program is unique because it helps children expand their skills in playful ways with games, puzzles, riddles, contests, and stories. The high-interest activities are informative and fun to do.

Home involvement is important to any child's success in school. *ENRICHMENT READING* is the ideal vehicle for fostering home involvement. Every lesson provides specific opportunities for children to work with a parent, a family member, an adult, or a friend.

AUTHORS

Peggy Kaye, the author of *ENRICHMENT READING*, is also an author of *ENRICHMENT MATH* and the author of two parent/teacher resource books, *Games for Reading* and *Games for Math*. Currently, Ms. Kaye divides her time between writing books and tutoring students in reading and math. She has also taught for ten years in New York City public and private schools.

WRITERS

Timothy J. Baehr is a writer and editor of instructional materials on the elementary, secondary, and college levels. Mr. Baehr has also authored an award-winning column on bicycling and a resource book for writers of educational materials.

Cynthia Benjamin is a writer of reading instructional materials, television scripts, and original stories. Ms. Benjamin has also tutored students in reading at the New York University Reading Institute.

Russell Ginns is a writer and editor of materials for a children's science and nature magazine. Mr. Ginn's speciality is interactive materials, including games, puzzles, and quizzes.

WHY ENRICHMENT READING?

Enrichment and parental involvement are both crucial to children's success in school, and educators recognize the important role work done at home plays in the educational process. Enrichment activities give children opportunities to practice, apply, and expand their reading skills, while encouraging them to think while they read. *ENRICHMENT READING* offers exactly this kind of opportunity. Each lesson focuses on an important reading skill and involves children in active learning. Each lesson will entertain and delight children.

When childen enjoy their lessons and are involved in the activities, they are naturally alert and receptive to learning. They understand more. They remember more. All children enjoy playing games, having contests, and solving puzzles. They like reading interesting stories, amusing stories, jokes, and riddles. Activities such as these get children involved in reading. This is why these kinds of activities form the core of *ENRICHMENT READING*.

Each lesson consists of two parts. Children complete the first part by themselves. The second part is completed together with a family member, an adult, or a friend. *ENRICHMENT READING* activities do not require people at home to teach reading. Instead, the activities involve everyone in enjoyable reading games and interesting language experiences.